What I Would Not Unravel

by Karen Lee Lewis

What I Would Not Unravel

by Karen Lee Lewis

Published by The Writer's Den

Buffalo, New York

What I Would Not Unravel

ACKNOWLEDGMENTS

Thanks to the editors of the following publications where some of these poems first appeared: *The Buffalo News, Slipstream, Artvoice, Traffic East Magazine, Letters to the World (Red Hen Press), Sacred Stones, Sugar Mule, Moondance, The Society, Hello/ Goodbye, The Shadow's Imprint, The Niagara Current,* and *existere.*

The poem "Even If" was nominated for a Pushcart Prize by Slipstream Press.

My most sincere thanks to The Banff Centre for my residency with The Wired Writing Studio. It was a blessing to be mentored by the spirited Don Domanski.

Many thanks to all those who gave me their honest and insightful comments when asked to read earlier versions of these poems, most especially my longtime writer's group companions—Maureen O'Connor, Amy Christman, Mary O'Herron and Jennifer Tappenden. Special thanks to Nora Gould for her generous and careful reading of this manuscript.

Cover art, "Draw", 2010, hand painted silk by Ginny O'Brien.

Published by The Writer's Den

www.garyearlross.com

Printed in the United States of America

ISBN: 978-0-557-33220-5

For Jessie and Shawn

Table of Contents

III

I

We are all fastened from earth
To the bellwether I sing

Scales of Time

Thank the scales of time for being
stiff and strong enough to bear
the balance. We wait
out the argumentative weights
the center easing into calm
lift quiet at the fulcrum.
Sometimes it takes years
sometimes half your life
until the still moment finally arrives
and then it hits you –
you are bound by the duty
of your breath to add another stone
to renew the oscillation, the uncertainty.
And so you look about your feet
where the next choice may lie
and you listen to the sound of birds
for something you might catch
to unearth a presence
whose substance will make
the remainder of your stay
worthwhile.

Waking Up with Arakawa and Gins

Even though my eyes are closed I can perceive
through opaque lids that the sun is cleaving
the horizon creating both daybreak and nightfall
the transitive light adhering and cutting a trajectory
of tangerine shadow

For as long as I can remember every morning begins—
with attempts to observe my own invisibility, an insight that
originates somewhere within the movement of my body's self
and with meditations on the sizelessness of thought
which I know is absurd and can't be measured but still I strive

I record my awakening impressions, storing them within
coiled filaments (the feel of warmed sheets) (the voices
of sparrows' wings as they skip points toward me)
they aim their feathered songs into my open window
into my closed eyes

I look forward to pulling the morning into my body
almost as much as I love pulling the night in, observing how
the back of my eyelids hold the aurora in abeyance
projecting vision within the blank, spending time
in discovery, walking myself through transparency
charting links between initiative and action
the day already underway

Sunrise

Salmon spawn strewn
from salt-tipped wings
of ancient erne and crawe

An uphill flow
freshwater influx
of Coho, Chinook, Chum

My riparian life—
foraging among gravel and grass
bones and flowers
where I find the lowest point
of sky

Blood rising
against the back of night's
black bear

Caught By the Light: A Cento

For Margaret Atwood

Hello, hello.

One woman leads to another,
the chandeliers aren't talking.

Who sends us these messages,
oblique and muffled,
for those who listen with their eyes,
tell me what it is for?

Confess: it's my profession.
The words I clench -
words fertilize each other,
language of the roots of rushes tangled,
mouth full of juicy adjectives.

I am amazed.
I am snow and
space, pathways.

We follow you
scattering floral tributes,
we are learning to make fire
(*tanulunk tüzet rakni*),
magic.

There is not much
time and time is not
fast enough for us any more,
traffic shifts back.
If we make stories for each other,
you make them new each time,
you trying to think of something
you haven't said,
making use of what
there is.

We need each others
breathing, warmth, surviving
is the only war
we can afford.

Call it *Please*. Call it *Mercy,*
of ink, twisting out into the clearness.

The steel question –
mark turns and opens,
where do the words go?
What can I give her?

Years ago you were caught by the light,

cut out of magazines

in another land.

It would be so good if you'd

believe,

the publicity.

The relationship is symbiotic,

indispensable.

At the last

judgment we will all be trees.

Dark-eyed Junco

Sky jumper, thistle seeker,
your heart is not worth the bother
of the sharp-shinned hawk.
What kind of meal could you make?
He would expend too much
to devour such tremulous meat.

But the neighbor's cat?
Might she carry
a little more beauty
in her growl
if she inhaled
your cloud belly
filled with seed?
She could make a soup
of your bones in her mouth.

You are ceaseless frittering.
Cold has faded your feathers
from black to gray.
Your wings flutter,
eyelashes in wind.

Buddha's Garden View

We don't believe
in dragons anymore,
Zen points mind
toward a garden.
Walk the circumference
letting stone speak
clear to heart.
Sand will sing
seven toned scales.
Difference permits relationship:
asymmetry allows symmetry,
is reciprocal gold.
Value the spaces,
air in/air out.
Power is lonely.
In mountain storm
poet Muso sits,
an isosceles flower,
mirroring original face,
a Buddhist dragon,
master of endlessness.

Word Cairn
For Robinson Jeffers

"Rock

Lovely

Oh"

Balance

Building

Waves

Human

Feel

Rock

Upon

Rock

We

Place

Time

Tower

Hawk

Sky

All Stones Are Broken Stones.

James Richardson

        All sounds

                move

        Stones receive this

          —music—

.

        slow

        time

          broken

                     into

                pieces

        Stones compose us.

Cathedral Bells

Sedona, Arizona, 2006

Cathedral Rock is ringing
birch responds   listing toward the sound
juniper knots   the desert floor
branches twisting like frayed rope

At the base of mountain   Creek speaks
her skin lays bare   a fortune of currency
porous collections of past torrent
lining the bank   visitors raise these smooth coins
creating innumerable cairns

Wounds   recede   return
iron blood fades   flesh   befriends
ashes   make peace   with gray
invest   in these colors
small and large victories   family
trust   balanced in each other

Attach declivity   of setting sun
green reflections   turgid shadows
attach weight of relationship
difference   complexity   pitch of expectation
attach root in rock   water in stone

foot in red sand   palm of hand

attach order in chaos   tumble of reason

silence   in mouth

Yearning   source of seek and gather

circular words   like awe and reverence

among caverns of sky   white buffalo clouds   streaming coyotes

infinite compositions of symmetry

Flight to Life

Flock of nine blue jays
July sapphires rising heat
one red cardinal

Mallards beat their wings
against the water's surface
my dog flaps her ears

Renegade cascade
starlings mass across the grass
leaping fleas on skin

Cowbird cowboy drops
imaginary pebbles
mentions "Guadeloupe"

Kingfisher on branch
slapping fish from side to side
lunch break over creek

Grey imposters hide
out in wild apple tree blooms
catbird camouflage

Three orioles' spoil
torn trumpets litter the ground
beautiful butchers

Hawk's talon withdraws
from dove's sunning stone body
giving flight to life

Over My Shoulder

the day's face
autumn hovering   suspended in stems
one year later knee deep in the mulch
of memory   I am surrounded
by a helpless hierarchy of unreachables
wounded veterans of disaster
asymmetrical   arboreal   amputees

Do the sparrows remember the storm
descending how agitation grew
miniature mountains rising
they could not fly   cave of forsythia
lost all shape of autumn   collapsing
into green white coffin

Do the muskrats remember
being shaken awake by roots
cursing trees ripping apart the night
ominous oracles unleashing
a thunderous thrashing
an ambush of falling
crystal machetes

Do the deer remember
crashing branches disemboweling
dementia of sound fracturing
stockpiles of arms   legs   trunks
Do they remember our faces
disbelief rising floodwater
crushed apricot   crimson   pumpkin
the brown water blushing with loss

Blue spruce remembers
The October Storm as its infallible hour
proving able to carry the weight
holding steady   an avalanche

Young Japanese lilac remembers
her indelicate trauma
too offended to bloom in June
she spent her time
cultivating forgiveness

This year recovered   less color shouting
like geese practicing formation
their cries a testimony against complacency
they spread cautionary tales
against a wall of mutinous sky
over their shoulders Lake Erie's trebuchet

quietly gathering warmth

catapult filled with ammunition

a liquid arsenal

amassing herds of Trojan clouds

We are clusters of soft maple shields

                we must yield

The Rapacious King

Chances are she saw him coming,
and maybe she slowed, just a bit,
to discern if he was the correct shade of orange,
and if the brightness of his spots were arranged
according to the ancient map divine
that tethers her invisibly
to gray-blue skies.

He tackles her,
pushing her toward the ground—
no graceful invitation here,
no consent required—
her wings spread flat against the dry meadow grass.
The creek's reflections trip and fall and
rise like smoke among the needled pines.

They enfold each other,
Monarch face to Monarch face,
cologne of loosestrife exhilarates.
He struggles to find her abdominal lair
amid clasping appendages.
He lifts her skyward
through yielding air,
the most beautiful flower of his days.

They alight within arms of oak
and remain joined
until the next sun climbs.

Attachment beckons separation.
Like a hawk he'll navigate
thermal longitudes gliding
in search of Michoacán refuge,
land of sugar cane and fir.
Unable to return to the kindling branch
she'll resume her milkweed junket,
where she'll work at laying down
the next generation
of honeycombed moons.

Regret We Plant Ourselves

Defenseless against my own naiveté
I planted the root of Asclepias
Milkweed: Greek cure
For the heart

Needy for life-giving restoration
I dreamt of Monarch's
Gold-flecked chrysalis
Admired milkweed's sturdy stems

I hatched a plot
For honeycombed eggs
That might grow more brightly
A summer's delight

Underground the milkweed spread
Her dark lineage a secret passage
In their beds the cream roots grew
Thick and deep and well

Milkweed leaf lured tussock moths
Aphid nurseries colonized
As ants harvested sweet secretions
Between wasps and next the flies

Earwigs hid from drunken spiders
Their trapeze nets a ripe buffet
Of corpses and spinnerets concealed
In dusky flower's eye

Feast of sugar coated bees
Milk of toxicity
This thrumming mess an infestation
My beds unkempt reveries

Grief is a haunted catacomb
I let the Trojan nightmare in
Desiring Monarch
Alone

I began to unearth this wild delusion
To bite back the sting with equal resolve
Raising the roots of my mistake
Hanging this sorrow up to dry

The compost pile grew higher by day
Time lost to heart's cure was measured by night
Regret supplanted my reckless indulgence
I returned to earth my need for flight

Wild Turkey

The sky expands
across your cheeks
as your harem drifts
stepping out in nervousness

You are deep dark fusion
of dusk and dawn
an unlikely tree knot
of oak backed sheen
glistening green

That kabuki mask
those burnt black eyes
sear memory into mine

Rust belt roots
a bronze aged belly
such an earthy bird

You wouldn't think it true
that I would miss
the wind wedged within
your folded feathers
the comical conical
on your hairy horned head

the way that brittle beard obtrudes

pink stem of thorny leg

rose singing spur

You tilt your fan

this way and that

corralling wall

of blazing heat

I bristle

at the future

the press of houses

spreading

the inevitable

loss of you

Pine Siskin

on a pillow of snow

his wings a whisper

of the sea's glass surface

and the sandy shore

engravings left

when the water pulled

its edges in

My Reluctance

has taken the shape of orchid

content to sleep

with green for years.

II

The resonance of relationship
is told in a story of thirteen sounds

Young Model to Cezanne

I am not an apple

I have more

dimension

than you can see

with that brush

Do not cut me

into pieces

but render me

transparently

Repose

She lies before him
an exhaled apology
Her mouth is his heart
glossy and beating
His breath disperses
her being
Dust becomes him
settling against the page
A new angle of repose

She and He

She is made of white noise

He is a fog filled meadow

Here the sacred nestles a gray divide
where white is black and black is morning and
morning layers the light like tail feathers in a down draft

She is a pulse of whitewater blood

He is transparent kindness, a smiling xanthic chimera

If she can be described as joyous, sleeping silence
then he must be, strictly speaking, comfortable noise,
an aftereffect of something breaking

She is the distance that slides
from one vertebra to another

He is a revolving spine of nights

The space between them cannot be erased
it is a consolation   they have grown

Close Cover Before Striking

It was not a trivial pursuit.
The burners on my stove wouldn't light.
Turning the knobs brought only the slow rush
of odor, not the ardor of flame.

I reached for a match box,
shaking it, to wake the inert
lip-stick dipped, rough hewn tinder.
Next the easy glide of interior, revealing
the sparkling garnet and glue. The grit
waiting to be cut, one against the other.

I admit a rare pleasure at the weight
of certain friction, the anticipation of ignition,
the pulling scratch-snap, the blue-orange dress,
the smothering blow, the intoxicating smolder,
the brief sulfurous dream.

I am this match of love and light.
Venus before sunrise. Philo and lumen.
A Philuminist—collector of loco-foco—
self-lighting bearer of phosphorous muse.

Like mates that eat from the same table
of incandescent elements this burning Lucifer
is a sacred marriage of heaven and earth.

I'm in no hurry to fix the stove.
I rather prefer this fertile need
to create a cosmos of light
with the strength of my hand.

Coat of Arms

I learned to speak the language of don't
touch me at my mother's side

My father used to joke
his tongue a fuller's teasel—raising bristle—
that the thistle was my mother's favorite flower

Her Scottish skin spread pink poison of embarrassment

I lay low in the weeds   earth's green urchin
while they passed back and forth
a martyr's frame wrapped in brambles

Some memories pierce through years
my father taught me—
harm a thistle   wound yourself

There is something humane about making obvious
what is disagreeable   to wear your power
to defend or offend on your sleeve for all to see

Field cactus stiff with cat's claw and spider legs
thistle combs the sky   raking clouds
holding safe the seeds of down
delivered into the beaks of goldfinch
their sweet songs flying over
my mother's coat of arms

What Sound

There is something to be said
for frugality in language.
How many sounds
do we really need
to mate for life?
What sound for follow?
For love that crosses
the long passage
between two bodies?
For a pair of Canada geese
the resonance of relationship
is told in a story of thirteen sounds.
Some think thirteen unlucky
yet the number unites
one's duality with three's divine grace.
What sound would you choose
for contentment? What sound
embraces child? Can you
imagine a different sound for laughter?
What about something foul,
the way stress makes a goose hiss
displeasure—her long neck
more snake than throat.
What sound for the endless

calling you'll make
when one day you lose
your mate?

So much to be said—
in stead the body's language
can attend to silence moving
moments that manifest
true partnership.

Geese often bow their heads
in a gesture resembling namasté—
I recognize the universe
within you.

In Thailand they pronounce
this motion
Why;
one small syllable
can make
a world.

Pointillism:

Her thoughts pixilate. She speaks in pin points and ellipses …
wants you to sign on the dotted line to surrender to her point of
view.

Once she punctured her extremities. Stippled poinsettias
suggesting pink petals on the tapering tips of her fingers and
toes. Each day was a garden walk. She never needed to cut
flowers. She showered with flowers, dried herself with flowers,
pleased herself with flowers.

She bloomed all year calling to mind Christmas scents…
mincemeat apple-walnut hot butter… a trio of tarts. She liked
to sew popped corn garlands and wrap them around deciduous
trees. She dropped trails of the crisp kernels in snow and named
them vanishing points.

She developed a habit, entirely useful, of stiffening her index
finger like a dog's taut tail. She trusted her fingertips would
lead the way; they became an essential detail that completed a
set of directions. She liked to drum her fingertips against the
thin skin of her wrists while considering questions… a bouquet
of moments… or a momentous bouquet?

She never believed that life was pointless. She was reminded of death at every turn. Her mother's premature point of no return left her terminally marking pauses—which became the punctuation of the dead. Red poinsettias were her mother's funeral shrubbery—faded plastic *wish you were here's* on a grave she didn't tend. She preferred to remind herself of livelier points of departure. Like Seurat's paintings her indelible inks were indivisible, they were a still point to which she could always return.

Prayer for Dawn

One lump
is not sugar to the body as to tea.
My friend discovers this—
finds it nesting under cover of skin.

Medicine jumps at what it knows—
choreographing tests
as the idea of cancer leaps
like brush fire among friends.

Only to love
doesn't seem enough.

How to dissolve
the malignancy of bitterness,
to soothe the body of our feeling?
What came first, the body or the dance?

What belief persuades the body
to perform a miracle?

Frail Grace

Her pain cannot be relieved
dehydration reigns   flesh time
balanced by water and salt
everything about her thinning
corpus diminishment

Winged vertebrae
seek soft landing
within ribbed cage
consumption accumulates
her body   weathering
summit of scapula disintegrating
femur, ligament, cartilage, fascia—
an *archaic torso*

It is not heartbreak   that will
thrust her over the threshold
a century of matriarchy
has taught her to withstand
its threadbare ways

She is a frail grace
solemnly shaped
by fusion and loss

the once terse mandible

known for proffering

blistering vesicants

now opens   in solitude

she is on her way

to the door

her pale hand holding

the railing firmly

slippered footfalls

soft as petals

fortified by sun

I watch the burning

wick cool

to brittle black

the burnished

liquid wax

growing concave

as it stills

this must be

what it's like

to die

you lose

the ability

to create a

reflection.

Hold Steady

1.

All I could say
was don't be afraid
Smoothing the lines on his forehead
Whiteness growing into him becoming him
Nurse quoting Horatio over his cracked heart
Calling all angels
How could she know he didn't believe?
Even I knew this was not the time
for poetry
She comforted herself at his expense
I sat next to him until I felt
able to leave his body
Realizing later on that I was not alone
Walking into the cool night air
I brought him home
so he could rest in silence

2.

Hold steady
Press hard enough
against the light switch

Force yourself

to wipe away

his finger prints

Transfer to paper

the memory

of his touch

3.

The canyon he left

keeps widening

Each day another inch

There is nothing

grand about it

Just space that grows

Within me today

it was wide enough

for a small deer

to pass through

4.

His thread bare dish towel

on my desk

White cotton with red stripes

worn to such softness
against his hand

Plaid lining from a trench coat
worn his last days like a vest
Chill heir to his body
Today it shoulders
the back of my reading chair

His quartz clock
continues counting strokes
Second hand a crystal oar
above the water line
His shadow floats
across the surface of sound
Time wearing away
Every minute
irretrievable

Dear Lydia,

Like a scarified seed
I was made to grow
quickly
surface scribed
my spirit scored like bread
time's crust   loosened

My mother gone   so long
she never left
a footprint in my homes

What use   to imagine
no wonder that
I always looked
transparent
climbing lines
the length of one
of my mother's white hairs
to reach   the observation point

I take out her soft white stole
that I keep   folded
like ambition
on a hanger in the closet

memory in vestment
this is my mother
what's left of my mother
saved   for special occasions
like this

I drape her stole around my shoulders
grasp the polarities   until the ends
unite across my chest
correspondence of chamfered edges
space cut   fitting me
to the beginning of her
my skin   her scarf
one epidermis

Given

A daughter's life
seedling settled into a private dominion
a latticework of loam, of root, of bone

In her the unseen working its favor
silken weaponry fertility demanding
her own right of way

Into a body of wonder she grows
whole with history

I give her to the weathered distance
of chance and circumstance
her exhalations white ellipses drifting

Against a backdrop of trees
I trace my years in Roman numerals
wishing to remain more than witness
to the chromosomes in the hour glass
to what I can and cannot contain
to live beyond my mother's years
lingering in my daughter's life
foreshadow born from my body's
opalescent husk

Sunday 1:02 PM

First one heron
then two rising
their strenuous pushing
against all that is grey
the way my son pushes
his long arms against me
reaching for the silver spoon
that cradle holding
a drop of our blood
I rock the air forward
every stroke an opening
fan of feathers
my fingers brushing
his hair

There are things

I do not choose

to leave

to chance

take you

for instance

I am squirreled

in a tree

droning

on on

danger treading softly

outside your view

Float

so that you may listen
to your body's ether
unfolding like linen
in waves

How

not to give anxiety—

that sharp-nailed colossus—

a slip a berth in our being?

How difficult to lie awake

attending it

a watchman in a lighthouse

of tempered glass

gulls' wings beating soft and tender

outside the biopsy of time

heavy like a washboard

held too many hours

Holding Back the Shadows

They lurk,

tap my shoulder and run,

ring my doorbell and disappear

behind laughing trees.

They are remnants

of my mother.

She stitched them

into her housedress pockets,

weighty things

the color of lead.

She passed them along to me,

when I wasn't looking,

too busy to see.

I try to sew them

into words

when I feel them

reaching for the light

in my daughter's eyes.

III

Sings of belonging
Sings of home

Spiral Born

In the folds of seascape
landscape   memory of light weight
spiracle idea framed with mind
nacre shelled nucleus of spirit
every round cell a buoyant bedchamber
for brackish eyes

Cretaceous ear to ground's clay pulse
listening to day's growing seedbody
humming crystal codes of Fibonacci
helix of sunflower kundalini
stems branch off to fill
the solar scaffold   a golden staircase
to a bronze star   no waste of space
in this garden

Earth is a spinning potter's wheel
circulating lodes of rain
indolent cephalopod kicks off his lotus lid
sinks like ram's horn into soil   holds on tight
long enough to become ammonite

Spiral incline of a wish
rolling within rolling without

molluscus rune of curves

breathes resurrection

sings of belonging

sings of home

builds evolution

revolution by revolution

To Wash Against

Everyday the rain

purple cast

thunder snapping

like wet towels

strung out clouds

dripping their Olympic weight

veins of an ancient lake

rising bulging pressing

against my alluvial plain

The Day Pulls

up its blue
stocking offering us
olives and bluegrass
we climb from sleep
slow and thick like honey
melt into the day's incline
we gather wild herbs
dig deep for potatoes
drink warm goat's milk
and dream often
of the Mediterranean
our amulet
a blueprint for living

Coyotes

wake us

package of howls

tucked like a lodestone

into early autumn nights

their cries a rippled surface

screech owl chiming

in from a distance

I can measure

with a breath

Jagged Notations

Sighing octaves of icebergs
jagged notations on a grand scale
spreading thaw   unsound
sheet music melting in glinting sun

Drifting   caesuras expand
green land creaking
like an out of tune cello

Cascade of carbon
dioxide dissolves
reshaping   uncertainties
saturating dissonance

Wind's instrument travels
a palette of pathways
gives rise to reverberant
    spaciousness
sea of moisture
sea of clouds
unknowing sea
musk of fertility

Underwater melodies

grow liquid identity

the world   dressed in wet

sackcloth and widow's weeds

surging volume embalms

There is always

something below—gravity sees
there is always
the weight of tomorrow today
a deeper force bending our knees
to carve a space for our unease
there is always

Pleasure or Memory

Regret craved company

and set the table

allowing Fear to sit at the head

He tried to mind everyone's business

Humiliation sent a wilting bouquet

Sin rested his tongue

of black licorice

After Grace spoke

Fear threw a wine glass

and smiled at all

the broken pieces

Splinter

I am the flaw
within you
buried sliver
of thought
a dark inclusion
you cannot reach
with your mind

Eventually
I will work
my way
free
and you will hold me
in your hands
and marvel
at my magnitude

To Have and to Hold

He is so used

to being invisible

that he paints

himself black

He dreams of being

abducted by someone

who can calm the terrors

of his doubt

He carries handcuffs

in his pocket

just in case

he finds someone willing

to take him

home

Unhinged

Sand flies straight	harsh grains	wear edges
saliva dries	words disappear	into
space		
Anguish crawls	interior (there, there)	constrictions
absences spread	(between) sounds	falling
away		
Sticky skin	peels	the sting
sentiment soothes	clouds rise	and
shatter		
Also	disintegration	rains
light arrives, uninvited	trees grow	meanwhile
apart		
Sleeping	memories migrate	(breathe)
scraping aside	soaring dreams	under
silence		

How to Jump Over Niagara Falls *or*
How to Become One
of the Wonders of the World

Don't leave a note. Go alone. All your life make people think that you don't like the water. Be exceedingly polite; beloved by fifth graders. Salt all fear. Do not be depressed. Do not be yourself. Take your medicine—don't take your medicine. Separate words into bit parts: believe, be, lie, belie, leave, eve….now scramble them. Select Independence Day. Swallow positive ions; love mist on your face. Water is a tight rope, grasp its invitation, it will help you unravel. See your heart turning colors, one minute it is black as a cormorant, the next white as a gull. Make sure you are out of harm's way. Quickly put one foot in front of the other. Let the water do the rest.

Vena Cava

Red gourd

red vase

rhythmic vessel

made brittle in the heat

of change

I am converted

into glass I watch

your knife enter

the right

atrium of my heart

Even if

After Adrienne Rich

Even if the woman was raped 96 times instead of 97
    and she was found years later   laughing under a tree
    her body a defaced limb   of history
    she would have the power   of growth

Even if my mother didn't die
    and she was found walking   without aids
    on a dirt road in Africa
    her shoulders chanting a soft chorus   with sun

Even if I had a cure
        for grief

Even if my father could sleep   through the night
    and his dreams   were not cinema verité—
    he would put his money down   for pornography

Even if it were free

Even if my mouth did not attract flies
    and I could   not speak
    inhumane words :

starvation, racism, fanaticism,

relentless atrocities   indifference

we might discover pieces

of hate

under our   fingernails

Even if beauty   didn't have an ulterior motive

and you could love me   whoever you and I are

it could be   something

What I Would Not Unravel

To lift   what is shed
a strand of horse hair
to bend it between branches   enveloping air
creating a boundary   a hem   an axis
that swirls like water on a drain's edge

To return to the horse   the earth
the brown horse the grey horse the Clydesdale
to coil their long threads into delicate rings
that sing from a common center   a weightless vowel
rising and falling

To bow to work   like a song
sparrow weaving a cradle   two inches diameter
to dwell within a clear circumference
to lay children there for safekeeping
wrapped   in a horse's mane or tail
that will dry quickly after a storm
that will fly when the wind is right

To walk towards me offering this
graceful whirl in the palm of your hand
what the world has loosened
you have gathered   in me

our infinite fragility

embedded in the course of days

love   a retreat

source of our belonging   here

this is what you have given me

what I would not unravel

Tunnel Mountain

Banff, Alberta, 2007

Train whistles in French
horn across the valley
Between you and I flies
an iridescent magpie
Reaching for the Bow's release
bones of bedrock fortify
mineral river lichen shivers
percussive pebbles murmur
flats and sharps whisper
chenille and corduroy

Shore lies drawing
on its memories
silent remnants
reflection the surface of
a tall peninsula
ready to swallow this stone
scribe whole

Between these lines of earth
scorching conduits fire
cataclysm channel avalanche channel
glacial crust scouring centuries

of slide and grind
that settle for the foot
of elk, coyote, deer and goat

The world is full of edges
some jagged some round
What is the difference
between subservience and reverence?
Gravity's knees are scraped regardless
crawling blind toward belief

Better to be a lodestone
of the sea listening
to the shape of water
and its promises to carry me
in its currents

Better to be ice
threatening relief over flow
Better to be dissolved slowly
and pulled into dangling
roots of Douglas Fir

Mouthed earth devours
scars reveal what
time conceals

When the time comes
for me to rise like mountains
I cannot hide myself in skin

When the time comes clouds
will drip into my mouth
I will hold my hands like pockets
life's blood will pine away years
recycling all kinds of green

When the time comes for trembling
aspen to bury themselves in sun
I will pack my spine with resolve
and the sheer veneer of days
I will not be able to grasp
how my self moves outward in all directions

When the time comes for me to grow bolder
to walk with a forest's sense of altitude
my eyes will turn to water
dutifully cleansing for the sights that follow
a small price to pay to breathe this air

My dreams a series of prefix reveal
I am always beginning

Pencil

Once you wake her up, she never sleeps. Pencil has her own relationship with the word erect. Descended from Chaucer, her name is a diminutive of penis 'tail.' She has a poet's core, her degrees of hardness formed by extremes of pressure. She was discovered sleeping under a fallen tree and quickly taken hostage by the government of England. When she was young she was treasured and smuggled by thieves. They used to call her 'Wad' and wrap her in sheepskin.

Like a man she looks best when shaved daily. She likes her points, she likes to make points, she is the point. When she undresses like a woman she leaves behind layers of twirled amber skirts. Pencil enhances femininity—eyes, lips, she is the horizon line.

Pencil loves to bare her interior, to leave messages on warm, wet tongues. She helps you write "I will not break/ the lead tips/ of my eyes." She has a nose for drama and an affinity for edicts; she is a connoisseur of cedar. Sometimes she makes mistakes on purpose. She doesn't worry about other pencils' feelings. She wishes she could lose herself every night in Einstein's hair, or find herself packed into the Hubble telescope for alien amusement. She travels without a parachute, or a safety net. If she breaks she doubles her pleasure.

Pencil doesn't like to be ruled and she doesn't need
to ask permission. If you rub against her she will take you anywhere.
She is a golden genie's lamp against your willing hand.

For a short time pencil feared her own obsolescence, when her splashy
cousins began multiplying like an inky virus. She knows she is often
taken for granted, or passed over for promotion, but she's come to
terms with the idea of erasure. She knows how it is. She whittles away.
Time made useful causes her to fade. It makes her harder to hold.

Notes

All lines/fragments for "Caught by the Light" used with permission, from Margaret Atwood's writings in various publications: *Procedures For Underground*, *Negotiating With The Dead*, *Quarry – March 1966*, *morning in the burned house*, *power politics*, *Crystal Garden*, *Selected Poems 11 – 1976-1986*, *Cries of the Spirit*, *Brick, fall 2001*

In the poem "Caught by the Light" the line "*tanulunk tüzet rakni*" is the Hungarian translation for the line that precedes it, "we are learning to make fire".

The aphorism by James Richardson appears in *Vectors: Aphorisms & Ten-Second Essays*. Used with permission.

The poem "Buddha's Garden View" is for Norris Brock Johnson, and was inspired by his article "Gardens of the Heart" in *Parabola*, Vol. 26:1.

The poem "Word Cairn" was inspired by a photograph taken by Karl Bissinger entitled "Robinson Jeffers at Hawk Tower", Carmel, California, 1950.

Photo by Jessica Lewis

Karen Lee Lewis was born and raised in Welland, Ontario, Canada, and now resides in Western New York. *What I Would Not Unravel* is her first full-length poetry collection. Karen works as a Teaching Artist for various non-profit organizations and art galleries, and teaches adult and youth writing workshops. Her "Picturing Poetry" project (with photographer Amy Meza-Luraschi) was the subject of a documentary by filmmaker Jon R. Hand. Her editorial and feature work for *Traffic East* magazine is archived at www.trafficeast.com.

LaVergne, TN USA
09 February 2011
215760LV00001B/5/P